T0353704

JESUS *in the* WORKPLACE

Understanding Jesus's Impact on Contemporary Work Culture

SANDRA M. CARTER

WESTBOW
PRESS®
A DIVISION OF THOMAS NELSON
& ZONDERVAN

WestBow Press books may be ordered through booksellers or by contacting:

WestBow Press
A Division of Thomas Nelson & Zondervan
1663 Liberty Drive
Bloomington, IN 47403
www.westbowpress.com
844-714-3454

Cover photo by Brian K. Sugden

ISBN: 979-8-3850-4309-5 (sc)
ISBN: 979-8-3850-4310-1 (e)

Library of Congress Control Number: 2025901369

Print information available on the last page.

WestBow Press rev. date: 01/28/2025

CONTENTS

CONTENTS

PREFACE

Throughout my career in the business world and my personal study of the Bible, I discovered that Jesus has profound insights about the workplace. His teachings are filled with stories that reflect principles still relevant today—truths that, when applied, have the potential to bring about meaningful change in the way we work and interact.

In today's fast-paced environment, professionals are constantly navigating challenges and pressures. My goal in creating this study guide is to introduce readers to Jesus, who fully understands the demands they face. This guide is designed with a simple structure and thoughtful questions, making it accessible to individuals regardless of their background or prior knowledge of the Bible.

However, no exploration of Jesus's teachings would be complete without acknowledging his greater mission as the Messiah. My hope is that through this study, readers will not only discover valuable principles for the workplace but will also encounter Jesus as the life-transforming Savior who offers solutions to humanity's deepest needs.

Thank you for joining me in this journey of reflection and discovery.

INTRODUCING THE STUDY

Today the world shrinks from absolute truth. Yet we rely on many unshakeable beliefs to successfully navigate our ordinary days. Unless we make our home on a space station, gravity, inertia, and momentum all affect us. Most of us enjoy dessert and would find poison more than distasteful.

The Bible, to those individuals who have a relationship with Jesus Christ, is the actual word of God. Many people regardless of their faith or lack thereof recognize that Jesus's teachings are worth consideration. What Jesus said and modeled represent truths, which when followed yield great results.

As contemporary workers—professional, blue collar, homemakers— what can we learn from a Jewish teacher living in first-century Palestine? Before his public ministry as a rabbi and teacher, Jesus followed his stepfather's profession as a carpenter. His close relationships included business owners, fishermen, women of independent means, and a reformed prostitute. Later followers included a literal tentmaker, doctor turned journalist, priests, seamstresses, teachers, prison wardens, and itinerant preachers. Jesus was acquainted with high government officials and often dined with businessmen who after meeting Jesus reformed their dishonest ways.

The work world offers growth, satisfaction, and fulfillment. With these benefits, workers today face uncertainty, stress, relational challenges, and questionable ethics. Weighed down by unreasonable demands and a general lack of appreciation, we can feel desperate and trapped. Does the Bible have some encouraging truths for us? It does!

Not only does Jesus have empathy for us but he also has a message of Good News that transforms our lives. He calls us to a new purpose, empowered by supernatural power and informed by a greater wisdom.

This study is designed to help participants understand that Jesus identifies with their workplace struggles and offers wise principles in response. Through the Bible passages, we learn about the person of Jesus Christ and his ultimate calling as Messiah.

The first five lessons, designed to fit a thirty-minute discussion, introduce Jesus as a participant in the workplace. The sixth lesson focuses on Jesus's true vocation, the Messiah.

Lesson 1: Jesus the Tradesman
Lesson 2: Jesus the Leader
Lesson 3: Jesus the Employee
Lesson 4: Jesus the Coworker
Lesson 5: Jesus the Wage Earner
Lesson 6: Jesus, the Messiah

Each lesson offers insights into the culture of Jesus's day, providing context for the principles found in the scripture passages. Participants need no previous familiarity with the Bible to consider the discussion questions, and all lessons include biblical references from the English Standard Version of the Bible.

As we study Jesus and the principles he taught, may we become instruments of transformation in our workplaces.

HOW TO USE THIS STUDY

Lesson Introduction

Each lesson begins with an explanation describing the cultural context of the scriptural text for the discussion.

Discussion Questions

Readers are directed to consider the scriptural passages referenced in this section and to answer the questions related to the text.

Getting to Know Jesus

This section provides additional context to better acquaint the readers with Jesus Christ as portrayed in the Bible.

For Further Study

The scriptural passages referenced in this section offer further insights into the lesson topic and also the character of Jesus Christ. (The referenced text is not included in this guide.)

Takeaways

The two questions in this section encourage readers to reflect on the lesson and to apply the principles in their workplaces.

Personal Reflections

This section presents the author's personal reflections on the lesson topic and highlights its relevance to current workplace situations.

JESUS THE TRADESMAN: TEACHER, RABBI, PROPHET, OR CARPENTER?

The world knows Jesus by many titles: rabbi, teacher, prophet, and king. Yet so much of Jesus's teaching revolves around the everyday demands of making a living, dealing with poverty, and managing wealth. We find Jesus visiting more often with tax collectors, fishermen, landowners, tradesman, homemakers, and merchants than the professional religious or political crowds.

During Jesus's day, Rome governed Galilee of Palestine, the region where he spent much of his life. The inhabitants faced major socioeconomic upheaval under the Romans. To fund their own lavish building projects and expansionist designs, Rome levied heavy taxes on their conquered territories. They employed local men appropriately called "tax collectors" to collect and deliver the monies. Rome allowed these men to exact more than the tax amount from the populace as compensation for their work.

The small farmers, under the burden of excessive taxation, sold their little plots to pay taxes or forfeited them, as did tenant farmers unable to repay their loans. Thus, wealthy individuals, many who were foreigners, took control of more and more land, forcing tenants and former owners to work as day laborers on these wealthy estate farms.

Fishermen took advantage of the Sea of Galilee and Jordan River to build businesses around their trade, sometimes employing laborers to assist them. Shepherds and goatherds, longstanding vocations in Israel's history, moved closer to the growing cities, sometimes supplementing their incomes by helping landowners harvest their crops.

It's little wonder that in this context we find that Jesus's followers Matthew and Mark ascribe a rather ordinary title to him. As a carpenter, Jesus followed in the footsteps of his stepfather, Joseph, and likely worked as an apprentice for six years beginning as early as age ten. In his day carpenters not only made household items such as furniture but also made wheels, boats, wagons, and other things constructed from wood.

Carpenters also worked on crews to build houses, towers, and bridges, among other large projects. These jobs often required these craftsmen to move from one construction site to another. Before Jesus ministered as a rabbi (religious teacher), he likely traveled with Joseph to various towns around the Sea of Galilee.

Could Jesus have had more in common with the average worker than the revered local priest? Is it possible that Jesus can relate to the challenges we face on the job—such as dealing with unrealistic expectations, operating with integrity, and meeting economic challenges?

Let's read what Mark, a disciple or early follower of Jesus and the author of the Book of Mark, wrote in Mark 6:1–3 to learn about Jesus's vocation.

DISCUSSION QUESTIONS

> He went away from there and came to his hometown,
> and his disciples followed him. And on the Sabbath
> he began to teach in the synagogue, and many who
> heard him were astonished, saying, "Where did
> this man get these things? What is the wisdom
> given to him? How are such mighty works done
> by his hands? Is not this the carpenter, the son of
> Mary and brother of James and Joses and Judas and
> Simon? And are not his sisters here with us?" And
> they took offense at him. (Mark 6:1–3)

The world has given Jesus many titles, but seldom do we hear him
called a carpenter. Yet both Matthew and Mark remind us Jesus,
until he began his public ministry, made his living as a tradesman.
Many contemporary workers make career changes. Jesus, at age
thirty, left the workbench to become a rabbi. Could he identify with
our vocational adjustments?

1. How did Jesus's friends and relatives know him (verse 3)?

2. Why were they surprised? Why do you think these people were
   offended by Jesus's teaching (verse 3)?

3. How would you feel if your childhood friend, the car mechanic's boy, started holding scholarly lectures at city hall?

4. How might Jesus's work as a laborer and small business owner for over two decades have prepared him to become a religious teacher?

5. What obstacles do you think Jesus may have faced in his career change?

6. How does knowing Jesus worked as a carpenter in his father's business help you relate to him?

GETTING TO KNOW JESUS

It's amazing that Jesus so identified with men and women that his closest associates recognized him simply as "the carpenter." Yet scripture tells us he was much more.

In John 4:25, Jesus spoke with a Samaritan woman, and she said, "I know that Messiah is coming (he who is called Christ). When he comes, he will tell us all things," to which Jesus responded in verse 26, "I who speak to you am he."

What did he mean? The Messiah, as the Old Testament prophesied, would come to reconcile people to God. Many people in Jesus's day, living under the oppression of the Roman Empire, anticipated a military leader who would defeat Rome and rescue his people. But the Messiah had a greater purpose and a kingdom under the authority of God himself. The Messiah would come, not just as a man, though he would be fully man, but also as the Son of God, God himself in the flesh.

FOR FURTHER STUDY

Read the following Bible passages to learn more about Jesus's birth and his life prior to the beginning of his public ministry: Matthew 1:1–4:17; Mark 1:1–12; Luke 1:1–4:13; John 1:1–34.

TAKEAWAYS

What is one thought or principle you could apply from this lesson to your work environment?

What is one new thing you learned about Jesus from this lesson?

Ask the experienced rather than the learned.

—Arabian proverb

PERSONAL REFLECTIONS

I've held jobs in a variety of workplaces—from retail to software as well as several years as a full-time homemaker. What could Jesus—who lived two thousand years ago in a dusty, impoverished region halfway around the world—offer me? Could he understand my situation when my female boss told me I didn't need a raise because I had a husband? Did he relate to my frustration when caring for three babies under three years of age and fearing my education meant nothing? Would he relate to my angst at returning to the corporate world after a twenty-year hiatus?

What challenges are you confronting in your work environment? And what decisions are you facing? A possible job change? The need for additional training? Your questions will differ from mine, but as you learn more about Jesus, I trust you will see that he not only relates to your challenges but he will also meet you in them with understanding and hope.

JESUS THE LEADER: LEADERS, SHEPHERDS, AND SERVANTS

Jesus was not politically correct; he didn't worry about following the cultural norms of his day. For example, in Jesus's day, Jewish men did not speak to women in public. Jesus not only spoke to women but he also stopped to address them directly, showing compassion for their difficult situations. Comforting a childless widow, pardoning an oppressed adulteress, and restoring an ostracized woman to society—all in public—flew in the face of both cultural norms and the narrow views of the religiously powerful.

Little wonder why Jesus modeled and challenged the concept of leadership. Where did he learn to lead? How did he develop his perspectives? Who were his role models? Jesus had occasion to see the good and bad in leadership. As a carpenter, he rubbed shoulders with other tradesmen as well as his wealthier customers. Living under the rule of Rome, he often observed and later suffered under the heavy-handed authorities.

Perhaps the most egregious example of leadership in Jesus's day was the politically correct and prominently connected religious sect called Pharisees. Jesus called them "whitewashed tombs" because they lorded their positions over others and used their authority to lay burdens on the common people. The Pharisees' interpretation of the Torah (law as outlined in the first five books of the Hebrew Bible) led to the oral law, a set of rulings given great weight among the people. Jesus criticized the Pharisees for observing the letter of the law rather than its spirit.

But Jesus had other role models too. These individuals held low positions on the totem pole of society; no one considered them leaders at all. Yet Jesus saw qualities worth imitating in them. Shepherds dotted the hill country surrounding Jerusalem selflessly, often at the risk of their own lives, caring for their precious flocks. They rescued their wayward sheep from vicious predators and moved their flocks to quiet waters because timid lambs would not drink from a moving stream.

In the city, slaves attended the households of the wealthy. These individuals had no representation, often living as foreigners in a hostile culture, the spoils of war. Some servants were Jews working off their debts. They did the most menial tasks, including washing the dusty, sweaty feet of the masters, their families, and their guests. The lives of slaves lay solely in the hands of their masters, and their well-being totally depended on their masters' discretion.

Read what John, another of Jesus's disciples, wrote in John 10:1–15 and John 13:3–5, 12–17 to learn about shepherds and slaves as unlikely models of leadership.

DISCUSSION QUESTIONS

"Truly, truly, I say to you, he who does not enter the sheepfold by the door but climbs in by another way, that man is a thief and a robber. But he who enters by the door is the shepherd of the sheep. To him the gatekeeper opens. The sheep hear his voice, and he calls his own sheep by name and leads them out. When he has brought out all his own, he goes before them, and the sheep follow him, for they know his voice. A stranger they will not follow, but they will flee from him, for they do not know the voice of strangers." This figure of speech Jesus used with them, but they did not understand what he was saying to them.

So Jesus again said to them, "Truly, truly, I say to you, I am the door of the sheep. All who came before me are thieves and robbers, but the sheep did not listen to them. I am the door. If anyone enters by me, he will be saved and will go in and out and find pasture. The thief comes only to steal and kill and destroy. I came that they may have life and have it abundantly. I am the good shepherd. The good shepherd lays down his life for the sheep. He who is a hired hand and not a shepherd, who does not own the sheep, sees the wolf coming and leaves the sheep and flees, and the wolf snatches them and scatters them. He flees because he is a hired hand and cares nothing for the sheep. I am the good shepherd. I know my own and my own know me, just as the Father knows me and I know the Father; and I lay down my life for the sheep." (John 10:1–15)

Sheep need a lot of care. Fearful and skittish, a lamb left to itself could lose its way, find itself on its back unable to regain its footing, or wander across the path of a hungry predator. Night was particularly difficult.

Shepherds had two methods for protecting their sheep. When near the cities, shepherds could leave their sheep under the care of a gatekeeper in enclosures called sheepfolds. These pens might house the flocks of several shepherds. In the open field, a shepherd would herd his flocks into a cave or other natural pen and lay himself across the opening as the "door" and security for his sheep.

1. What peculiar relationship do you see between the shepherd and the sheep in verses 1 through 5?

2. Who goes out of the gate first, the shepherd or the sheep? What significance does this observation have for leadership?

3. What might be involved in knowing the voice of your leader (boss, manager, CEO), and why is it important for leaders to know their reports well?

4. What are some differences between the hired hand and the shepherd? What are the implications for a leader who acts as a hired hand and a leader who operates as a shepherd?

> Jesus, knowing that the Father had given all things into his hands, and that he had come from God and was going back to God, rose from supper. He laid aside his outer garments, and taking a towel, tied it around his waist. Then he poured water into a basin and began to wash the disciples' feet and to wipe them with the towel that was wrapped around him.
>
> When he had washed their feet and put on his outer garments and resumed his place, he said to them, "Do you understand what I have done to you? You call me Teacher and Lord, and you are right, for so I am. If I then, your Lord and Teacher, have washed your feet, you also ought to wash one another's feet. For I have given you an example, that you also should do just as I have done to you. Truly, truly, I say to you, a servant is not greater than his master, nor is a messenger greater than the one who sent him." (John 13:3–5, 12–16)

In the Middle East of Jesus's day, everyone wore sandals and walked everywhere through dusty, muddy streets. Work animals such as donkeys, sheep, and cattle as well as wild dogs and cats shared the same thoroughfares.

It was customary for a hospitable host to instruct his slave to serve his guests by washing their feet as they entered his home. In this story, Jesus's host neglected his duty, and apparently none of the guests humbled themselves to do the dirty work. So Jesus, the honored guest as well as a recognized and respected rabbi, stepped into the shoes of a slave.

5. How would you have reacted to Jesus if you were one of the guests whose feet he washed?

6. Jesus knew he was nearing the end of his time with these disciples, his followers. What lesson was Jesus trying to teach them? Why was this leadership lesson so critical for them?

7. What do you learn about leadership from these verses?

GETTING TO KNOW JESUS

The coming Messiah was described in amazing detail by the prophet Isaiah, whose writings appear in the Old Testament book by his name. Prophetically, Isaiah—writing nearly 650 years before the birth of Christ—described the Messiah as both a shepherd and a servant.

The flock in this passage represents all who follow the Messiah. What will the good shepherd do for them? What did Isaiah say the Messiah as servant would do? Whose servant was the Messiah?

> He will tend his flock like a shepherd; he will gather the lambs in his arms; he will carry them in his bosom, and gently lead those that are with young. (Isaiah 40:11)

> Behold my servant, whom I uphold, my chosen, in whom my soul delights; I have put my Spirit upon him; he will bring forth justice to the nations. (Isaiah 42:1)

FOR FURTHER STUDY

Read Psalm 23:1–4 in the Old Testament portion of the Bible to learn more about the shepherd's care for his sheep.

TAKEAWAYS

What is one thought or principle you could apply from this lesson to your work environment?

What is one new thing you learned about Jesus from this lesson?

The key to successful leadership today is influence, not authority. Servant leadership flips the script on traditional management and places the focus on supporting the team.

—Ken Blanchard, *The One Minute Manager*

PERSONAL REFLECTIONS

Leaders come in all shapes and sizes. We've all known the type A personality who centers their life around the office to the detriment of a social life and expects the same from us. We all dread to work for the micromanager who metaphorically looks over our shoulders and asks pointlessly detailed questions. And how do we feel when our boss takes the credit for our success but manages to pass blame down the ladder?

Many years ago, as a young developer, I had a boss who rarely spoke to his employees, continually shifted priorities, and managed to move to the next level before the effects of his mismanagement became evident. I've observed that companies tend to promote individuals into management based upon qualities other than good leadership skills, and too often they leave new leaders to dog paddle at the far end of the pool. It's little wonder that statistics show most people leave a job because of a poor supervisor.

"Servant leadership" is discussed, but do we really know what it looks like? Jesus doesn't bother promoting himself nor does he "pull rank." Rather, he models for us what a leader should do; he serves, he brings focus and clarity to the mission, and he promotes the well-being and success of others. Where can we find leaders like Jesus today?

JESUS THE EMPLOYEE: FREEDOM FROM GOLDEN HANDCUFFS

Jesus likely apprenticed as a craftsman under his stepfather, Joseph. Scripture offers hints that Joseph's family was relatively poor. It is doubtful that Joseph employed any individuals other than his own sons. What would Jesus know about the struggles we face as employees? Would he understand the competition among coworkers, the ambition that tempts us to push others down to lift us up?

Scripture does not tell us much about Jesus's life as a craftsman working under the authority of his earthly father. But we see glimpses of the lessons he learned in many of the parables Jesus shared. For example, in Luke 16:10, Jesus says, "One who is faithful in a very little is also faithful in much, and one who is dishonest in a very little is also dishonest in much."

Jesus often used stories about the interactions of slaves and their masters to teach spiritual truths. Slavery in first-century Palestine covered a wider range of master/slave relationships than the disgraceful form later practiced in Europe and the United States.

A slave in Jesus's day might refer to an indentured servant working off a debt or a bonded laborer as well as the traditional definition of a slave.

But in his stories regarding these employer/employee relationships, Jesus also highlighted the value of faithfulness, resourcefulness, and loyalty. One such parable describes a businessman and three of his servants. Jesus says the man must leave his home for a lengthy period of time. In preparation for a long absence, he calls three servants and entrusts various amounts of money to each man. He wants them to invest the money wisely and deliver a profit to him upon his return.

Jesus shared this story to teach his followers lessons about the kingdom of God. But in this story, Jesus also has lessons for us in the workplace. What qualities do we see Jesus value in an employee? What does this story tell us about Jesus's view of the employer/employee relationship?

Read Matthew 25:14–29 from the New Testament to learn what Jesus valued in a good employee and how these three servants did or did not display these traits. Colossians 3:22–24 share another important truth. (The biblical book of Colossians is a letter the early follower of Jesus Paul wrote to a fledgling first-century church in Colossae.)

Note:

Talent is the equivalent of approximately twenty years' wages of a common laborer of the day. Jesus is using exaggerated amounts to make his point.

Parable is a story illustrating a spiritual or moral lesson.

DISCUSSION QUESTIONS

"For it will be like a man going on a journey, who called his servants and entrusted to them his property. To one he gave five talents, to another two, to another one, to each according to his ability. Then he went away. He who had received the five talents went at once and traded with them, and he made five talents more. So also he who had the two talents made two talents more. But he who had received the one talent went and dug in the ground and hid his master's money. Now after a long time the master of those servants came and settled accounts with them. And he who had received the five talents came forward, bringing five talents more, saying, 'Master, you delivered to me five talents; here, I have made five talents more.' His master said to him, 'Well done, good and faithful servant. You have been faithful over a little; I will set you over much. Enter into the joy of your master.' And he also who had the two talents came forward, saying, 'Master, you delivered to me two talents; here, I have made two talents more.' His master said to him, 'Well done, good and faithful servant. You have been faithful over a little; I will set you over much. Enter into the joy of your master.' He also who had received the one talent came forward, saying, 'Master, I knew you to be a hard man, reaping where you did not sow, and gathering where you scattered no seed, so I was afraid, and I went and hid your talent in the ground. Here, you have what is yours.' But his master answered him, 'You wicked and slothful servant! You knew that I reap where I have not sown and gather where I scattered no seed? Then you ought to have invested my money with the bankers, and at my coming I should have received what was my own with interest. So take the talent from him and give it to him who has the ten talents. For to everyone who has will more be given, and he will have an abundance. But from the one who has not, even what he has will be taken away." (Matthew 25:14–29)

1. What did the businessman do prior to leaving on an extended trip?

2. Why do you think he gave differing amounts to each servant? What does this tell you about the employer's knowledge of his servants?

3. How might the businessman's example inform managers as they hand out responsibilities?

4. What did the employer discover when he returned? What do you think he expected?

5. How would you describe the attitudes of each of these three servants toward their responsibilities? Toward their employer?

6. What does this passage say makes a desirable employee? An undesirable employee? What happens to those who are not faithful in the little things (verse 29)?

> Whatever you do, work heartily, as for the Lord and not for men, knowing that from the Lord you will receive the inheritance as your reward. You are serving the Lord Christ. (Colossians 3:23–24)

The third servant had a dim view of the character of his employer. He also put his security in his master. In today's business world, organizations often rely on "golden handcuffs," the promise of future compensation or ownership, to retain talent. This false security, this hope of future significant reward, can tempt us to forsake integrity or to feel trapped in uncomfortable situations in order to cling to these benefits.

In addition, we don't have the luxury of choosing our supervisors. Like the servant in the parable, we may regard our bosses as harsh, demanding, or inadequate, and we often do not have control over our direct reports. Would it surprise you to know the top reason most employees choose to change jobs is a poorly performing manager? But the Bible says we can choose who we ultimately work for.

7. Who does the apostle Paul say we should work for? How would Paul's instruction in Colossians 3:22–23 free us from the restraints of golden handcuffs?

GETTING TO KNOW JESUS

Jesus as the Son of God had every right to be served in amazing and spectacular ways. He could've claimed a right to be the ultimate authority. Yet God chose to send his Son to experience life from birth to death fully as a man. He sent Jesus to serve us, identifying with servants over masters. Mark 10:45 says, "For even the Son of Man came not to be served but to serve, and to give his life as a ransom for many."

And Jesus submitted himself ultimately to his Father's will, even in the face of suffering and death by crucifixion. Matthew 26:39 says, "And going a little farther he fell on his face and prayed, saying, 'My Father, if it be possible, let this cup pass from me; nevertheless, not as I will, but as you will.'"

The Messiah suffered to obey the heavenly Father and to serve us. What do you learn about Jesus as the obedient, sinless Son of God?

FOR FURTHER STUDY

Read Philippians 2:3 and James 3:16 in the New Testament section of the Bible to see the dangers of selfish ambition; read Proverbs 18:12 and 22:4 in the Old Testament and Philippians 2:3–11 and 1 Peter 5:5 in the New Testament to see the value God places on humility.

TAKEAWAYS

What is one thought or principle you could apply from this lesson to your work environment?

What is one new thing you learned about Jesus from this lesson?

> Be a yardstick of quality. Some people aren't used to an environment where excellence is expected.

—Steve Jobs

PERSONAL REFLECTIONS

Ah, those golden handcuffs. Though the term seems dated, it is still a very real part of the corporate world. In his many years as a corporate executive, my husband had occasion to see individuals wearing golden handcuffs abandon their integrity or abuse others to retain those glittering incentives.

Like the character Gollum in *The Lord of the Rings*, these people sought the promise of future reward, failing to consider the cost to themselves, their families, and sadly, to their integrity. My husband, who trusted his career to the Lord, was free from those shackles and earned a reputation for his honesty and hard work.

Maybe you don't have stock options dangling before your eyes, but what are you striving to obtain? What incentives do you need to work faithfully and with integrity? Who ultimately do you work for?

Lesson Four

JESUS THE COWORKER: WATERCOOLER DISCUSSIONS AND OFFICE POLITICS

Jesus worked in the family business, which has its own unique challenges. By the time Jesus began his ministry, Joseph, the family patriarch, had died. As the eldest son, Jesus may have trained his siblings and worked alongside them. Later, Jesus began a movement with a diverse group of individuals—tax collectors, fishermen, and a follower named Judas who used his position to embezzle from the group's fund and later betrayed Jesus to his enemies.

Most of us do not work independently; we often operate as team members. Strong teams include individuals of varied skills and personalities, people who fill gaps in others. As humans, we prefer to relate to individuals like us. Team members' differing skills, personalities, perspectives, temperaments, experiences, and agendas can prompt conflict and stifle progress.

Aren't we all tempted to think we could do a better job than a peer? Do we wonder why the boss promoted a coworker who didn't pull their weight? Who hasn't been tempted to manipulate situations to

JESUS IN THE WORKPLACE

elevate oneself and downplay others' achievements? It's tempting to judge coworkers' attitudes or actions based on what we assume about them or a situation. Assumptions often lead us down twisted paths. Rarely do we know all the facts that lead us to the truth. Would we want others to judge us by our own standards?

Jesus's followers faced similar temptations. Jockeying for position, these men could not imagine what lay in their futures. All but one paid for his loyalty with martyrdom. As they walked with Jesus from town to town, they were yet unaware of the full implications of their new vocation. During much of their time with Jesus, these men thought he would conquer Rome and offer them positions of authority.

Jesus was a keen observer. The Bible tells us in several passages that Jesus knew the thoughts of men; he knew what was in their hearts. While modeling his work ethic for his followers, Jesus also identified and addressed some of the weaknesses that might later destroy their effectiveness. What did these men need to understand to effectively continue Jesus's work after his death? As you review the passages in this lesson, look for the issues that could derail both the disciples and your team.

These truths, though simple in concept, are challenging to apply. How might we transform our workplaces by obeying a few basic commands?

Read Matthew 7:1–5, Matthew 20:20–28, and John 21:20–22 to learn a couple of principles Jesus teaches about relating to others, particularly coworkers.

DISCUSSION QUESTIONS

"Judge not, that you be not judged. For with the judgment you pronounce you will be judged, and with the measure you use it will be measured to you. Why do you see the speck that is in your brother's eye, but do not notice the log that is in your own eye? Or how can you say to your brother, 'Let me take the speck out of your eye,' when there is the log in your own eye? You hypocrite, first take the log out of your own eye, and then you will see clearly to take the speck out of your brother's eye. (Matthew 7:1–5)

1. In Matthew 7:1–5, what does Jesus mean when he says, "The measure you use it will be measured to you"? (Hint: In the Lord's Prayer, Jesus prayed, "Forgive us our debts as we also have forgiven our debtors.")

2. How would it look if you applied your own criticism of a coworker to yourself? How would it change your behavior?

3. Why do you think Jesus used the example of a log versus a speck in the eye? (Did you know this line came from the Bible?)

Then the mother of the sons of Zebedee came up to him with her sons, and kneeling before him she asked him for something. And he said to her, "What do you want?" She said to him, "Say that these two sons of mine are to sit, one at your right hand and one at your left, in your kingdom." Jesus answered, "You do not know what you are asking. Are you able to drink the cup that I am to drink?" They said to him, "We are able." He said to them, "You will drink my cup, but to sit at my right hand and at my left is not mine to grant, but it is for those for whom it has been prepared by my Father." And when the ten heard it, they were indignant at the two brothers. But Jesus called them to him and said, "You know that the rulers of the Gentiles lord it over them, and their great ones exercise authority over them. It shall not be so among you. But whoever would be great among you must be your servant, and whoever would be first among you must be your slave, even as the Son of Man came not to be served but to serve, and to give his life as a ransom for many." (Matthew 20:20–28)

4. In Matthew 20, we see a doting mother make a request for her sons; what did she want? Do you think she thought of this request herself? (In the Middle East, the seat to the right hand of the host is reserved for the most honored guest.)

5. Do you think these brothers understood the cup (God-appointed destiny) Jesus would drink? What important information might we miss when vying for promotion?

> For not from the east or from the west
>   and not from the wilderness comes lifting up,
> but it is God who executes judgment,
>   putting down one and lifting up another.
> (Psalm 75:6–7)

We look for promotion in many different directions, from mentors, colleagues, and supervisors. We try to know the right people to move up the career ladder. But the psalmist tells us who is ultimately in control of our situations.

6. According to Psalm 75:6–7, who ultimately is in control of our promotion? How might this truth change the way you view your job status?

> Jesus said to him, "If it is my will that he remain until I come, what is that to you? You follow me!" (John 21:22)

7. Prior to Jesus's remark in John 21:22, Jesus had intimated that Peter would die a martyr's death. (Tradition says Peter died by crucifixion.) Peter, looking at the disciple John, asked Jesus whether John would die similarly. What did Jesus say to Peter? Why is this good instruction for us too?

GETTING TO KNOW JESUS

Jesus often turned things on end, calling his followers to live "totally other" from the world's norms. Put others first. Forgive seventy times seven. Treat others as you want to be treated. Love your neighbor and pray for those who persecute you. Give. Serve. Mourn. Make peace.

Self-promotion had no place in Jesus's world. He trusted the Heavenly Father to lead, guide, protect, and provide. "God confidence" leaves no room for elbowing our way to the front of the line. But trusting in God in our work frees us to take risks, to make excellence our standard, and to promote others who do a good job.

FOR FURTHER STUDY

To learn more about the character Jesus values in his followers, read the Matthew 5:2–11 from Jesus's famous Sermon on the Mount.

TAKEAWAYS

What is one thought or principle you could apply from this lesson to your work environment?

What is one new thing you learned about Jesus from this lesson?

> Whenever a man has cast a longing eye on offices,
> a rottenness begins in his conduct.
>
> —Thomas Jefferson

PERSONAL REFLECTIONS

I worked at a software company with a brilliant yet cantankerous coworker. He once remarked, "We would be just fine if it weren't for our customers!" We laugh, but from time to time we've all thought, *I'd be just fine at my job if I didn't need to deal with the other employees.*

If our coworkers would just do their jobs the way *we* think they should, wouldn't we be more successful? And then there's the employee who is so obviously climbing their way to the next level, clamoring for promotion over more qualified peers. Who do they think they are?

I love Jesus's comment about the log in the eye. When we find ourselves judging a coworker, could that same criticism be said of us? Scripture tells us to make it our ambition to lead quiet lives and to mind our own business. How different would our workplaces look if we pursued *that* kind of ambition?

JESUS THE WAGE EARNER: FUNDING THE BUCKET LIST

Taxes, savings, 401K, and retirement income are just a few of the concerns for today's wage earners. Taxes seem too high. There's not enough paycheck at the end of the month to stash into savings. Should we contribute to a 401K? Will we retire with enough income to maintain a comfortable lifestyle, to check off the items on our bucket lists?

Could Jesus understand a wage earner's concerns? Jesus was self-employed as a craftsman and later lived as a rabbi supported by his followers. He rubbed shoulders with fishermen, tax collectors, and wealthy property owners. He observed, he listened, and then he taught. Jesus used the experiences of the workers of his day to not only teach spiritual lessons but also to address those individuals' concerns.

In the midst of addressing these subjects, Jesus challenged the status quo. Jesus, never satisfied with shallow responses, insisted on digging into the heart of an issue. A rich young man approached Jesus to assert his righteousness and find out what he could do to please God. Jesus, aware the man was making an idol of his wealth, told him to give all his money to the poor. (Read Matthew 19:16–26 to learn the rich young man's response.)

The self-righteous Pharisees frequently tried to discredit Jesus. In one particular situation, they attempted to squeeze Jesus between the Jews and their Roman occupiers. The Romans insisted the Jews pay a healthy tribute to the Roman Empire, a source of intense irritation to the Jews. One day the Pharisees approached Jesus to ask, "Is it lawful to pay taxes to Caesar, or not?" With incredible wisdom, Jesus took a denarius, the coin of the day, and asked his oppressors whose likeness appeared on its face. When they answered "Caesar's," Jesus gave his now famous response, "Render to Caesar the things that are Caesar's, and to God the things that are God's."

Don't rely on your riches to impress God. Obey civil authorities; pay your taxes. But did Jesus talk about preparing for retirement and enjoying the fruit of our labor? You may be surprised that he did! Using the hypothetical example of a successful landowner, Jesus shares a story to teach a lesson about amassing wealth for our old age. In this simple parable, he offers perspective on the role of financial savings in our lives, challenging us to consider a short-sighted sense of security.

Read Luke 12:13–21 to see what Jesus says about a rich fool.

DISCUSSION QUESTIONS

Someone in the crowd said to him, "Teacher, tell my brother to divide the inheritance with me." But he said to him, "Man, who made me a judge or arbitrator over you?" And he said to them, "Take care, and be on your guard against all covetousness, for one's life does not consist in the abundance of his possessions." And he told them a parable, saying, "The land of a rich man produced plentifully, and he thought to himself, 'What shall I do, for I have nowhere to store my crops?' And he said, 'I will do this: I will tear down my barns and build larger ones, and there I will store all my grain and my goods. And I will say to my soul, "Soul, you have ample goods laid up for many years; relax, eat, drink, be merry."' But God said to him, 'Fool! This night your soul is required of you, and the things you have prepared, whose will they be?' So is the one who lays up treasure for himself and is not rich toward God." (Luke 12:13–21)

At first blush, the rich man's actions seem prudent. Isn't it good to save for retirement? Don't we want to be independent in our later years? Jesus is not promoting irresponsibility; we do need to be good stewards of our finances, but if we put our security in our finances alone, might we find ourselves greatly disappointed?

1. What is the situation that prompts Jesus to tell this simple story (verse 13)?

2. What do you think Jesus means when he says one's life does not consist in the abundance of one's possessions?

3. How does this concept relate to our views of identity and individual worth?

4. What did the rich man do when he had bumper crops?

5. What did this rich farmer not anticipate?

6. Why do you think Jesus is critical of his actions? What did Jesus call him?

7. Is Jesus criticizing saving and financial prudence? How might reading this story change your attitude toward your personal wealth?

GETTING TO KNOW JESUS

Jesus has an uncanny way of calling us to loosen our grip on things of this world. He particularly challenges us not to lash our security to our finances. The apostle Paul in one of his letters to his student Timothy puts it this way, "The love of money is the root of all kinds of evils" (1 Timothy 6:10).

In Matthew 6:19 Jesus tells us not to store up treasures for ourselves on earth. Perhaps he had the foolish farmer in mind. While Jesus does call us to be prudent and to handle our financial resources wisely, he makes the bold statement in Matthew 6:19–34 that it is *impossible* to serve God and wealth.

Read Matthew 6:35–34 to learn who will provide for our needs. How does this understanding take the worry out of life?

FOR FURTHER STUDY

Read Matthew 5:25–34 and 1 Timothy 6:17–19 to learn the proper attitude toward our material goods and what we should consider when saving for our futures.

TAKEAWAYS

What is one thought or principle you could apply from this lesson to your work environment?

What is one new thing you learned about Jesus from this lesson?

Do not boast about tomorrow, for you do not know what a day may bring.

—Proverbs 27:1

PERSONAL REFLECTIONS

If you google how much savings you need to retire, you will get a variety of answers. Here are three of them:

- Save ten to twelve times your annual salary for your retirement.
- Plan to have an annual income in retirement equal to 80 percent of your preretirement annual salary.
- Accumulate enough money to withdraw 4 percent annually from your retirement fund without depleting the savings.

Whatever plan we follow, we can find ourselves putting the security of our future into our savings. We may outlive our fund or not need it for nearly as long as we anticipated. Like the businessman in Jesus's story, we don't know how long that fund needs to last or how much money unplanned circumstances will require.

We do need to exercise discipline and responsibility in the management of our finances. Respectable money managers encourage us to have an emergency fund and to save and invest our resources. But Jesus knows the length of our days. Maybe we should ask him what we will need and trust his leading day by day. What would it look like for you to plan for retirement with Jesus?

JESUS, THE MESSIAH: KING OF KINGS AND SUFFERING SERVANT

Jesus at various times held different vocations—craftsman, teacher, rabbi. But the Bible tells us he held one position from before time began, and he will hold that title into eternity. The Bible says Jesus is the Messiah, the Anointed One, the Son of God.

Skeptics find this role of Jesus extremely troubling. A craftsman? Yes, we can identify with a carpenter. A teacher? We still quote him, his wisdom resonating with each new generation. A rabbi? This title seems a bit of a stretch for his detractors, but he was a Jew, and he did teach. He had followers, and crowds gathered to hear him speak.

But Messiah? How would we even recognize a messiah? Many men made that claim, yet no one actually held the title for long. Some Jews still look for the Messiah to come; others gave up long ago, writing off prophecy about an anointed one as an outdated notion or a fanciful myth. Yet the Bible is one story from beginning to end. In the Old Testament, through the words of his prophets, God describes the Savior to come. The New Testament reveals the

Messiah and how he conquered sin and death for all who put their faith in him.

Scholars point to over three hundred Old Testament prophecies fulfilled by Jesus. The prophet Micah in Micah 5:2 predicted the Messiah would be born in Bethlehem. Hosea, in his prophetic book, said the Messiah as a child would spend some time in Egypt (Hosea 11:1). The Old Testament prophet Isaiah in beautiful poetic language describes the Messiah in interesting detail. Yet what do we do with these biblical predictions? Was Isaiah written after Christ died rather than before his advent as the Bible claims?

Many dismissed the credibility of the Book of Isaiah until the discovery of the Dead Sea Scrolls in 1947. Hidden in clay jars in a cave in the present-day West Bank of Israel, Hebrew manuscripts dated 150–100 BC contained most of the Old Testament books, including the Book of Isaiah. The Book of Isaiah records only some of the many Old Testament prophecies concerning the Messiah. Isaiah tells us we can recognize the Messiah as a "Wonderful Counselor, Almighty God, Prince of Peace" (Isaiah 9:6).

Yes, the Book of Revelation in the New Testament describes Jesus as "King of Kings and Lord of Lords." But the prophet Isaiah detailed another vision of this Anointed One. Isaiah portrayed the Messiah in a surprising light as a suffering servant.

Read Isaiah 53:1–7, 11 to see Isaiah's profile of the Messiah.

DISCUSSION QUESTIONS

Who has believed what he has heard from us?
    And to whom has the arm of the Lord been
    revealed?
For he grew up before him like a young plant,
    and like a root out of dry ground;
he had no form or majesty that we should look
at him,
    and no beauty that we should desire him.
He was despised and rejected by men,
    a man of sorrows and acquainted with grief;
and as one from whom men hide their faces
    he was despised, and we esteemed him not.

Surely he has borne our griefs
    and carried our sorrows;
yet we esteemed him stricken,
    smitten by God, and afflicted.
But he was pierced for our transgressions;
    he was crushed for our iniquities;
upon him was the chastisement that brought us
peace,
    and with his wounds we are healed.
All we like sheep have gone astray;
    we have turned—every one—to his own way;
and the Lord has laid on him
    the iniquity of us all.

He was oppressed, and he was afflicted,
    yet he opened not his mouth;
like a lamb that is led to the slaughter,
    and like a sheep that before its shearers is silent,
    so he opened not his mouth.

Out of the anguish of his soul he shall see and be
satisfied;
by his knowledge shall the righteous one, my
servant,
make many to be accounted righteous,
and he shall bear their iniquities. (Isaiah 53:1–7, 11)

1.   What do we learn about the servant in Isaiah 53?

2.   Isaiah says the servant was "marred, beyond human resemblance"
     (Isaiah 52:14). How does this verse predict Christ's experience?
     (See John 19:1–3 below.)

Then Pilate took Jesus and flogged him. And the
soldiers twisted together a crown of thorns and put it
on his head and arrayed him in a purple robe. They
came up to him, saying, "Hail, King of the Jews!"
and struck him with their hands. (John 19:1–3)

Note: Flogging required beating the prisoner with a whip made
of several leather straps that had sharp shards of bone and metal
embedded in them. While the Jews stopped a scourging at forty
lashes, the Romans imposed no limit.

3. How is the servant described in Isaiah 53:2–3?

4. What does Isaiah say about the servant's role in Isaiah 53:4–6?

5. What does Isaiah say about us ("we") in Isaiah 53:4–6?

6. How did the servant react (Isaiah 53:7)?

7. What does Isaiah say the servant will do for those who recognize him (Isaiah 53:11)?

GETTING TO KNOW JESUS

Today we are often associated with our vocations—engineer, homemaker, accountant, electrician, etc. Our acquaintances describe us by the ways they interact with us. Jesus, too, was known to the individuals of his day by various roles—craftsman, rabbi, and even prophet. The Jews of his day looked for a political savior, a warrior who would free them from the tyrannical rule of the Roman Empire. The religious leaders saw Jesus's popularity as a threat to their power and influence. The poor and oppressed wanted a king who would care for their needs. Even his most ardent followers, his disciples, did not fully understand his identity as God come into the world in human flesh.

But Jesus had a particular role he wanted to be known by. When Jesus asked his disciples how they, as opposed to the crowd, recognized him, Peter replied, "You are the Christ, the Son of the living God" (Matthew 16:16). Jesus wanted all people, Jew and Gentile, to know him as the Christ, the Messiah.

The entire Old Testament pointed to the coming of the Messiah who would save his people from their sins. Jesus fulfilled over three hundred Old Testament prophecies concerning the Messiah, but this Messiah would not be an earthly king. He would conquer sin and death, rescuing Jew and Gentile from eternal separation from God. By the sacrifice of his own life, he would reconcile flawed humanity to Holy God. And by miraculously rising from the dead, Jesus guaranteed that same resurrected life for all who trusted in him.

When Jesus asked his disciples how they recognized him, Peter replied, "You are the Christ, the Son of the living God" (Matthew 16:16).

If Jesus asked you, "But who do you say that I am," how would you respond? What would it mean in your life if you knew Jesus as the Messiah?

FOR FURTHER STUDY

As workers, we can learn much from the truths Jesus taught. Jesus has empathy for us, and he also has a message of Good News that transforms our lives. He calls us to a new purpose, empowered by supernatural power, informed by a greater wisdom, and in relationship with the one who gave his life to redeem us and reconcile us to God.

Read John 3:16.

Who is Jesus to *you*?

TAKEAWAYS

What is one thought or principle you could apply from this lesson to your work environment?

What is one new thing you learned about Jesus from this lesson?

He is no fool who gives what he cannot keep to gain what he cannot lose.

—Jim Elliot (Martyred in 1956 in Rio Curaray, Ecuador, while attempting to share the Good News of Christ with the Waodani people)

PERSONAL REFLECTIONS

I'm convinced we were made to work; work gives us joy and satisfaction. But we will also wrestle with challenges and difficulties. The Book of Genesis describes creation and the Fall of humanity into sin, a life of rebellion against God. I find it interesting that God gave Adam work to do while Adam was still without sin. Work was good for Adam.

But Adam's disobedience brought judgment from God, who said man would work by the "sweat of his brow" and continually fight "thorns and thistles." We will always find ourselves facing office politics, poor leaders, difficult assignments, and often, too little pay at the end of the month. Thank you, Adam.

I had the wonderful experience of working for a boss who put the principles of Jesus into practice. Was he perfect? No, but he infused joy, integrity, selflessness, and excellence into the culture. God has a better plan for us. He provided Jesus to deal with our sin problem, to reconcile us to God the Father, and to help us live differently. With Jesus, work can prove more joy than sorrow. Following his lead, we can be agents of transformation in our workplaces.

Appendix

THE GOSPEL

The "Gospel" means "Good News," particularly the news that Jesus is Lord and Redeemer, the solution to our sin problem. Here are the key points of the Gospel[1]:

- **Jesus is the Lord.**
  o Jesus Christ is holy God who came to earth born to a human mother but fully God and fully man. He is the supreme authority over everyone and everything.

- **Jesus will restore the world with regard to the problem and effects of sin.** (Sin is the rebellious attitude toward God and the behavior prompted by that rebellion.)
  o All men and women have a sinful nature and cannot approach a holy God until a sinless sacrifice has paid the penalty for their sin.

- **Jesus Christ is the one and only Savior of sinners.**
  o Jesus Christ, the sinless Son of God, paid the penalty for sin through his crucifixion and resurrected to life; Jesus defeated death for all who put their faith in his saving work.

---

[1] Adapted from Scott Lothery, *Always Good News*, Christian Focus Publications Ltd, 2023.

- **Jesus saves all sinners who by grace (the unmerited favor of God) put their faith in his saving work, acknowledging Jesus Christ as Lord in their lives.**
  - To sinners saved by his grace, Jesus Christ gives the gift of his Holy Spirit to empower them to have a vibrant relationship with God and to live godly lives. One day all believers will be raised from death to enjoy sinless, eternal lives with God.

To put your faith in Jesus Christ as your personal Lord and Savior and enjoy a relationship with him, pray something like the following:

Jesus, I believe you are the promised Messiah, Lord of all. I admit that I am sinful. I know I have not recognized God's authority in my life and his love for me. As a result, I have not lived a life that is good and right.

I need a savior, and by faith I acknowledge you are the Savior I need. I rely on your death to pay for my sins—past, present, and future. Saved by your grace, your unmerited favor, I commit my life to you, receive the gift of the Holy Spirit given to all who believe, and stand secure in the power of your resurrection; I place my hope in living eternally with you. I look forward to living my life in relationship with you. Amen.

If you put your faith in Christ, record the date in your Bible and tell a friend about your decision to follow Christ.

Steps to growing in your relationship with Jesus Christ:

1. Pray and read your Bible daily. (Suggestion: Start by reading the Book of John.)

   a. God communicates with us through his Word, the Bible, helping us learn more about him and his plans for us.

   b. We share our hearts and needs with God through prayer. ACTS is a simple acronym describing the key elements of prayer:

      i. A—Adoration: Praising God for who he is.

      ii. C—Confession: Acknowledging sin restores our relationship with God and allows him to make us more like Jesus (1 John 1:9).

      iii. T—Thanksgiving: Thanking God for all he has done and is doing.

      iv. S—Supplication: Sharing your heart with God and asking him to supply your needs and the needs of others.

2. Attend a church that is committed to teaching the Bible and honoring the Good News of Jesus Christ.

3. Talk with your pastor about baptism, the public profession of your new faith.

4. Connect with a small group of people from your church to study the Bible together.

5. Find a friend who has a mature relationship with Christ and ask them to mentor you in your new faith.

ABOUT THE AUTHOR

After retiring as a product manager in the software development industry, Sandra Carter and her husband, Garry, returned to Barrington, Illinois, from the San Francisco Bay Area. She deeply values her roles as wife, mother of four, grandmother of five, and an active member of her church. Sandy enjoys visiting local coffee shops and takes great pleasure in welcoming family and friends into her home.

Printed in the United States
by Baker & Taylor Publisher Services